FREEZE DRYING COOKBOOK FOR PREPPERS

How to Freeze Dry, Preserve and Stockpile the Right Foods for Up to 25 Years to Survive Any Crisis in The Safety of Your Own Home

RAYMOND L. HILLMAN

Table of Contents

Chapter 1
Introduction to Freeze-Drying

What is freeze-drying and where do its origins lie?

Freeze-drying (lyophilization) is the process whereby a product goes through a dehydration process, involving freezing, a drop in pressure, and removal of ice. The water contained in a product moves from a solid to a gas, avoiding the liquid state.

During the process, because a low temperature is used, the resulting factor is a product that not only has its taste and appearance preserved but also its nutritional value. This is due to freezing preventing changes in the product's physical state, delaying any deterioration, extending its life, and enabling the rehydrated product to be in a very good state.

Therefore, the art of freeze-drying, although it has its uses in the wider world, its use and role in preserving food has proven to be essential and an invaluable tool for the prepper.

In terms of time scales the art of freeze-drying is not a new development, as its origins stem back to as early as the 13th century when the Incas noticed that over time food that was kept at high altitudes would firstly freeze and then dehydrate. This was discovered when they stored potatoes high in the Andes Mountain peaks. They were subjected to freezing temperatures at night. During the day they would squeeze out the water from the potatoes and leave them in the sunlight to dry out.

This process developed for the preservation of blood products and medicine during World War two. Furthermore, it was NASA that took the art of freeze-drying to a new level, developing foods that would remain stable in space, whilst maintaining their nutritional benefits, shelf life, and a reduction in any bacteria or crumbs. Freeze-dried foods were developed in packages for ease of use and required just water to rehydrate for consumption.

Freeze-dried products are popular and convenient amongst hikers and are used as military rations and as meals for astronauts. Due to freeze-dried foods being much lighter than wet food, a greater volume of food can be carried. Also, freeze-dried food can be easily dehydrated with water if desired and the shelf-life of the product is longer than wet/fresh foods making them ideal to carry on long trips by hikers and military personnel and of particular use with astronauts as having no access to cook meals and storage is limited to carry many things. Freeze-dried meals for the astronauts are lightweight, space-saving, and have a long shelf-life for long missions.

With the knowledge obtained from researching the process of freeze-drying, the benefits for you and your family are endless. Knowing that you could support your family through a global event or just through a temporary food shortage must bring peace to your heart. And one of the best and most effective ways of achieving this is by freeze-drying produce to use when needed.

Freeze-dried foods are a healthy food choice. Due to its many beneficial factors, freeze-drying is one of the most common dehydration methods.

Whilst preserving the food's color, flavor, and structure, freeze-drying is one of the best ways to retain plant compounds and nutrients within the food.

In comparison with other drying methods, freeze-drying is the most effective at retaining antioxidants, like anthocyanins, flavonoids, and vitamin c.

In fighting off the harmful effects of oxidative stress in your body, antioxidants are very beneficial compounds. These compounds are widely found in most fruits and vegetables.

One of the reasons why freeze-drying aids in extending the shelf life of particular foods is that due to the decreased water content of the product, this in hand prevents the growth of molds, yeasts, and bacteria.

With some fresh plant-based foods not being available at certain times of the year, extending the shelf life of certain foods with the freeze-drying process means that these foods can be available at other times.

Finally, due to freeze-drying, a food's volume and weight will be reduced, thereby making it easier to handle, store and transport.

Now to discuss the freeze-drying process, as having a basic understanding of stages, methods, storage and use of these products is key to its success.

Chapter 2
Stages, Method, Storage and Rehydration

The four stages in the process of freeze drying

PRETREATMENT

With regards to food, this is about its correct preparation to ensure the success of the whole process. Although whole meals can be freeze-dried, some products require to be treated individually to achieve the best results and be properly prepared. When choosing your food item, always pick the freshest and wash thoroughly to remove any unwanted dirt, particles, and contaminants. This will ensure the result will be at its best when consumption takes place. Also cutting some foods into small pieces (such as fruit and vegetables) will help in the expulsion of water during the freeze-drying process.

FREEZING

The food product is frozen under atmospheric pressure. During this stage, the food is frozen often at a temperature below which the phases (solid, liquid, gas) that the item goes through exist. These low temperatures will ensure the item goes from a solid to a gas state, avoiding melting. This is fine for other items, but with food, it can cause ice crystals to form inside which would affect the texture and nutrient content of the food.

To avoid this the freezing process is done rapidly, taking the item below its melting point. This prevents the formation of large ice crystals thereby preserving the food item perfectly. A temperature of around -50 C (-58 F) to -80 C (-112 F) is often the chosen setting used.

PRIMARY DRYING

During this phase, the pressure is lowered to the extent that any frozen excess water is removed (known as the sublimation stage).

SECONDARY DRYING

During this phase, the pressure is normally lower and the temperature is raised to allow desorption drying to take place. This is where any remaining water is removed from the product and the item reaches its ideal humidity.

Methods of freeze-drying foods

Here we will discuss the most popular methods of freeze-drying your foods. It's about deciding which is the best method for your lifestyle.

FREEZE DRYER

If you have the means to purchase one of these then they are a great option for safely and effectively freeze-drying a wide variety of individual food items right through to complete meals. They come with several trays allowing you to freeze-dry many items at the same time.

To use:

1. Arrange the foods in the trays, ensuring they do not exceed the tray's height and any necessary space is left around the particular items.
2. Place the trays in the dryer and close the doors (see particular models as some have an insulating pad to insert before closing the doors).
3. Freeze the food at around -40 to -80 degrees C (please follow your individual manufacturers' recommendations).
4. Allow the processing time to pass (around 24 hrs.). Certain foods will take more or less time (please consult the guide you will receive with your dryer).

5. Once complete, transfer the freeze-dried product to a mylar bag and seal it with an oxygen absorber if specified.

Home Freezer

Anyone new to the world of freeze-drying may wish to start simply just by using their freezer/deep freezer.

To use:

1. Place the chosen food on a tray, ensuring evenly spaced.
2. Insert the tray into the freezer and set it to the lowest temperature.
3. It can take anything up to 2-3 weeks for the item to successfully freeze-dry.
4. Once completed, transfer the item into an air-tight storage bag and keep this either in your freezer or pantry.

Dry Ice

This is a much faster method than using the normal freezer, as moisture is evaporated quicker from the food by the dry ice.

To use:

1. Place the food in freezer-safe bags.
2. Put these in a cooler
3. Cover the bags completely in dry ice and leave for around 24 hours.
4. Once freeze-dried remove the bags and store them in your freezer or pantry.

Vacuum Chamber

This method is by far the costliest but also the most efficient way of freeze-drying foods. It involves a special vacuum chamber to freeze-dry the food, they work by speeding up the process.

To use:

1. Arrange the food to be freeze-dried on a tray, avoiding a mass of food together, and ensure it is evenly spaced.

2. Place the tray in a freezer until the food is solid.
3. Remove and transfer the food to the chamber at around 120m Torr and set the temperature to 10 degrees C.
4. The food needs to remain in the chamber for around a week for effective sublimation to take place.
5. When complete, remove and transfer the food item to an air-tight container to store.

Storing the freeze-dried food

When packaged and stored under the right conditions, freeze-dried foods can last up to 25 years in some cases. Proper storage is essential as the products will be susceptible to moisture, light, and heat.

We will discuss three main essential things that you must do to ensure you are storing the foods correctly.

MAKE SURE THE FOOD IS COMPLETELY DRY

To be able to successfully store your freeze-dried product you must ensure that it does not contain any moisture, which would cause the food to spoil and could greatly reduce the length of time that the item will remain edible.

You can test this by simply breaking a piece of the freeze-dried food in half and checking to see if it contains any water or ice particles. Also, if the item feels cold to the touch, then it needs to be placed back into the freeze-dryer for a further cycle.

Only then will storage of the item be successful to enjoy many years to come.

CHOOSING THE CORRECT STORAGE CONTAINER

There are various options on the market to store your freeze-dried foods.

Option 1.- Plastic bag

This should only be used to store foods for a very short length of time as they offer very minimal protection to the foods. Even freezer bags themselves are not much improved.

Plastic bags are thin, clear, and not air-tight making them susceptible to exposure to air, light, and varying temperatures, which ultimately will affect the freeze-dried food inside leading to its deterioration.

Therefore, although better than nothing at all, they are the least effective when it comes to storing your freeze-dried foods.

Option 2. - Glass container with lid

Airtight containers such as mason jars again are useful to store foods for a shortened length of time, or for foods that require storage but will be consumed regularly. These include foods such as yogurts, vegetables, and fruits. Without any further protection than the jar, these foods can successfully be stored in your pantry for several months.

The foods stored will not last long, because the jar contains oxygen that cannot be fully removed and thus shortening the life span of the food significantly.

When you have foods stored in these, if you open them to remove a piece of the contents you must remember to close the lid tightly afterward.

Option 3. – Vacuum storage bags

These storage bags are more effective as they are accompanied by a packing machine that removes the air within the bag before it is sealed. These bags are thick and very tough, designed to last longer than your average storage bag, but do let in light making them not as effective as some other options.

Once an airtight seal has been obtained these bags are successful in storing foods for an average of 1-10 years.

Option 4. - Mylar bags

If you're looking for a bag that can store an item of freeze-dried foods for lengthy periods, up to 25 years, then look no further than the mylar bag.

This bag is made from a clear polyester resin, which is attached to aluminum foil, therefore protecting its contents from any light, heat, or moisture. They are thin, lightweight, and flexible and be stored as fold up small. Despite this they are exceptionally strong, making them difficult to tear. Should you accidentally tear one then duct tape can be used to repair the hole.

They are widely available and a very popular choice amongst the prepper community.

They are available in different sizes, making them not only successful but also practical to meet all your storage needs.

They can be used alongside a sealer but also with an oxygen absorber which you pop into the bag before it is sealed and this will significantly preserve the contents for many years to come.

REMOVING ALL AIR AND MOISTURE

When it comes down to preserving foods, the two main enemies that affect this are air and moisture. To achieve a high level of sealed security for your product, you will require to remove as much oxygen as possible before closure.

Widely available and in different sizes to match the mylar bags are oxygen absorbers. These are designed to remove any residual oxygen that could be left in the bag before it is sealed.

Once the oxygen has been removed and the bag sealed then it can be stored knowing your product is in safe hands.

Locations such as your pantry, kitchen cupboard, or food storage box make ideal places to store the packages as they are best located in dark places, away from any light. Also storing in a stable ambient temperature is important as severe or excessive heat will ultimately affect its storage potential, lessoning the life span of its contents.

How to tell if freeze-dried food has degraded

With freeze-dried food, color is always a good sign to observe indicating its freshness. Any fading in the color is indicative of a change in flavor, freshness, and nutritional value. Although there could be a change in these factors, the food itself is perfectly safe to eat.

Tips for rehydrating freeze-dried foods

EAT THE FREEZE-DRIED FOOD DRY!

Freeze-dried foods can be eaten as they are, dry. Freeze-dried foods are easy to eat as they are crumbly, and not tough to chew.

Meats that are cooked and freeze-dried are great to eat as a snack. Dried vegetables and fruit are healthy and make great alternative snacks. Yogurt is another food that can be eaten freeze-dried and is delicious.

The only issue with eating too many freeze-dried foods is that as it has no water content you can get digestive problems so the occasional food is ok along with plenty of water.

AVOID OVERHYDRATING YOUR FREEZE-DRIED FOODS!

When rehydrating your freeze-dried foods, you need to avoid adding too much water. When you add too much water to the food and then drain off the excess water before consumption you will also end up removing some of the vitamins from the food.

When rehydrating foods, you only need a small amount of water enough to cover the base of the food, then gradually stir to reconstitute it. Extra water may be needed for meats.

DON'T ALWAYS HYDRATE YOUR FOOD FIRST

Sometimes it is best to rehydrate the ingredient for a recipe before adding it to your meal. This is true if your meal is not water-based, so the item should have water added to it first and then use it like a fresh ingredient.

DON'T OVERCOOK YOUR MEAT

Although hot water speeds up the hydration process it is wise to not use hot water when you're hydrating cooked meat. If you add boiled water to it, the result will be very tough meat. Therefore, it is best to use warm or cold water to rehydrate meat and then add it to the meal that you are preparing.

Chapter 3

Advantages & Disadvantages of Freeze-Drying

Advantages of freeze-drying

Because of the preservation of quality, characteristics such as aroma, rehydration, and bioactivity, freeze-drying is viewed as the main method of choice for dehydration of food. These characteristics are higher compared with foods dried using other techniques.

WHOLE FOOD NUTRITION

As a nation, we constantly seek nutritional information about the foods we consume. With freeze-dried foods being fresh foods that have gone through the process, they are generally free from synthetic, artificial, and highly processed materials.

Nutritional values can be listed on freeze-dried fruits and vegetables as they are real fruits and vegetables.

A food's nutrients and color are maintained due to the low processing temperatures used in freeze-drying, greatly decreasing any deterioration of the product. For example, freeze-dried fruit maintains its original shape and its soft crispy texture.

RE-HYDRATION

A dried product is considered to be of lower quality if it cannot be easily or fully rehydrated. Complete rehydration can occur in a food that has been freeze-dried because the product is porous. This show that the product was of great quality.

CUSTOMIZATION

This is where an individual can customize to their needs. Different sizes and shapes can be cut or ground into different freeze-dried foods. These may be from whole fruits and vegetables or even powders. The finished product can be mixed easily into any blend.

APPLICATION VARIETY

Food processors can incorporate real fruits and vegetables into many applications due to customization and blending capabilities. Categories of freeze-dried applications include breakfast ones, like hot and cold cereals, ready-to-eat snacks, beverages like smoothies, or whole fruit pieces added to beverages.

PROLONGED SHELF LIFE

There is a direct coalition between the moisture content of a product and its shelf life. The potential for bacterial growth is removed due to water being removed during the freeze-drying process. There is a variation in the moisture content of different products, but the average for freeze-dried products is around 3% moisture.

With freeze-dried products, the actual length of their shelf life varies according to their packaging, storage, temperature exposure, and of course the item itself.

VARIETY

Whilst plant-based products are the most popular foods to be preserved, there are a wide variety of foods that go through the freeze-drying process enabling the prepper to have a large selection of both individual and whole meals ready for whenever they are needed.

Some of the foods (although discussed more extensively later in the book) that can be freeze-dried include:

Fruits: oranges, bananas, pears, blackberries, apples, strawberries, raspberries, and fruit puree.

Vegetables: carrots, mushrooms, peppers, pumpkin, tomatoes, asparagus, etc.

Meats: beef, chicken, pork, turkey, fish, shrimp, eggs

Grains: rice, beans, pasta, quinoa, and polenta

Frozen meals: whole meals like stews, chili, stir-fries, and snacks

Beverages: milk, juices, coffee, tea, and instant drinks

Spices: ginger, mint, basil, garlic, and oregano

Sweeteners: maple syrup for sugar powder

Disadvantages of freeze-drying

On the whole, freeze-drying is an excellent method of preserving food for use in the short and long term. There are a few things to consider before you begin to freeze dry and a few precautions that you should follow to ensure that not only the result is effective but that you and your family are safe.

MICROBIAL GROWTH

Although microbial growth can be prevented by the low moisture conditions created by the freeze-drying process, some microbes can contaminate the foods as they can occur due to the low-temperature dehydration process in freeze-drying. This results in disease-causing microorganisms in raw foods surviving the drying process and can consequently be found in the stored food. This can lead to foodborne illness once consumed.

Although some foods can be freeze-dried raw, precautions need to be taken to ensure that the product has been thoroughly washed and the freshest product chosen to be freeze-dried so that no contaminates enter the freeze-dryer at the beginning of the process, limiting this occurring.

Some raw foods that require to be cooked before consumption may also need to be cooked before freeze-drying.

Although in the freeze-drying process, a food's antioxidant content is preserved, due to foods being highly porous this can allow easy access to oxygen. This can result in high levels of oxidation or degradation of bioactive compounds.

Silicone oil leakage

Within the freeze-dryer silicone oil is the most common fluid that is used to heat or cool the shelves. If there are any areas where there is damage or wear to the connections between the shelf and the hose, the continuous heat/cool cycle could lead to a leakage of silicone oil.

This in turn can lead to contamination of the product being freeze-dried leading to costly losses of the food/s being processed.

To help prevent this from happening mass spectrometers are used to detect vapors that are released by silicone oil so that immediate action can be taken to avoid contamination of the product within the freeze-dryer.

Cost

The cost of freeze-drying will ultimately depend upon the method chosen by the individual.

Freeze-drying on average costs around five times as much as conventional drying. Therefore, it is most suitable for products that increase in value with processing. Cost varies depending on the product chosen to freeze-dry, the packaging material, and the processing capacity of the machine, etc. During the process of freeze-drying, the most energy-intensive part is the sublimation and therefore the most expensive part. If a freeze-dryer is chosen to preserve foods, then although the initial outlay for the machine can be expensive, the capabilities of such a machine and its versatility could far out way the initial cost.

For the individual that wishes to preserve a wide variety of shelf-stable foods, particularly in large quantities, and wishes to store those foods for the long term the cost could be justifiable.

Time

Depending on your chosen method for freeze-drying, some methods take a lot longer to freeze-dry your foods than others. This needs to be taken into account, but ultimately the best method with regards to expense, practicality, and personal ability needs to be considered and researched before an informed choice can be made.

Chapter 4
Foods Suitable for Freeze-Drying

Freeze-drying has many uses in today's society. It can be used to preserve not only fresh produce from our gardens but also shop-bought foods. An extensive store can be made to be useful in times of emergencies, for camping and hiking trips, or just in prepping ahead to save time in the kitchen, a benefit to those with very busy lives.

Unlike other popular preserving techniques, freeze-drying has a clear advantage in that it helps foods retain their flavor, color, and nutritional values. Also, freeze-drying will not lead to any alterations in the size of the freeze-dried product from its initial state or any loss in texture.

Making the right choices and choosing the methods I covered earlier, if you are embarking on your journey in the world of freeze-drying then I can assure you it will be a journey to remember.

The possibilities are endless, enabling you to have a vast, delicious, nutritious supply of both individual foods, full meals, and snacks ready prepared for use in both the short and long term to feed you and your family. Also, in preserving the foods that you know, you are ensuring that when it comes to serving these meals to your family you will have the satisfaction of knowing that they will be ones that you will all enjoy and be of nutritional benefit.

Within the next section, I will discuss in more detail the individual foods that can be freeze-dried and those that either cannot or you will have difficulty with. Also, instructions on how to freeze-dry these particular groups of foods.

The list of foods is by no means infinitive, as you will discover with further research and often by experimenting on your own with foods and recipes that you and your family enjoy eating and that's where the fun begins!

I hope you enjoy your new culinary exploits in the world of freeze-drying, an adventure that all the members of your family can participate in enabling quality family time.

Many different types of foods can be freeze-dried for later use. Storing foods this way is ideal for the prepper wishing to have a supply of foods that can be used to make nutritious and tasty meals that the family will all enjoy, in the event of a man-made or natural disaster occurring, forcing them to take shelter and survive for an uncertain length of time, using the supplies they have prepared. Some of these foods that can be freeze-dried are discussed in the following chapter.

Foods that can be freeze-dried include:

- Dairy (cheese and milk)
- Fruits and vegetables (can be sourced from your garden or bought from a grocery store.
- Eggs (both raw and cooked)
- Meat (pork, chicken, turkey, beef, venison, etc.;
- Fish (both raw and cooked)
- Meals already prepared e.g., Lasagna, pasta, soups, etc.
- Desserts e.g., pies, puddings,
- Herbs and spices
- Drinks
- Other items

Dairy and Eggs

These include:

- Cheese
- Yogurts
- Milk
- cream
- Sour cream

- Eggs
- Ice-cream

Dairy products can be freeze-dried using different methods. Leaving a space at the top of your tray allowing for expansion during the freeze-drying process you can add these directly to a tray, or if you wish to make portions (handy for using in recipes) these can be poured into molds first, then placed on your freeze-drying tray. If you are freeze-drying ice cream then it is worthwhile choosing a well-made brand, as some cheaper makes contain air causing crystals to form in the final product which could alter the taste when you consume it.

Eggs are such a useful product to be able to store safely as they are used in so many recipes. Their adaptability and nutritional value are unquestionable. When freeze-drying eggs, crack the eggs directly onto your freeze-drying tray ensuring there is a space between them allowing for any expansion. (As for any product that you are freeze drying, please follow the manufacturers' recommendations on accurate freeze-drying times for whichever method you choose to freeze-dry your foods.) Once removed from your freeze dryer place the eggs in a sealed jar or bag to preserve.

Fruits and vegetables

Fruits that can be freeze-dried include:

- Blackberries
- Blueberries
- Bananas (sliced, with citric acid will maintain their color)
- Raspberries
- Apricots
- Slices of apple (plain or coated with cinnamon)
- Pears
- Pineapples
- Avocado (add lemon to maintain its color)
- Cherries (pitted and halved)
- Grapes

- Mangoes
- Kiwis
- Limes
- Strawberries
- Peaches
- Oranges
- Tangerines
- Watermelon

When freeze-drying fruits, the two most important things to remember are to thoroughly wash the fruit and only use healthy produce. Peeling and in particular cutting some fruits that have a thick outer skin e.g., blueberries and grapes, allows for the water contained within the fruit to escape during the process allowing the fruit to be preserved in great condition.

The fruits require to be either sliced, cut into chunks, or bite-sized pieces. Also, any stones removed. You must seal these in a mylar bag with an oxygen packet and they will maintain their nutritional value for many years to come. These can be used in desserts, added to cereals for a tasty breakfast, or just eaten as a healthy alternative for a snack.

Vegetables that can be freeze-dried include:

- Green beans
- Peas
- Beans
- Kale
- Broccoli
- Carrots
- Spinach
- Pumpkins
- Squash
- Mushrooms
- Onions
- Corn (remove from the cob)
- Celery
- Peppers

- Potatoes (thinly sliced are great for chips)
- Tomatoes
- Yams
- Zucchini

When freeze drying vegetables, again these need to be of good quality to achieve the best results from freeze drying and cut into portions of the same size ensuring the process is uniform. Once frozen these can be placed into an absorbent bag with an oxygen packet and again stored for years to come allowing you to make tasty, well-balanced meals for your family in the future.

Meats

Meats that can be freeze-dried include:

- Chicken (sliced, cooked, or raw)
- Minced Beef (best cooked to remove excess fat)
- Beef (cut up, or if left whole(steaks) allow extra time to reconstitute)
- Ham
- Pork
- Sausages (linked or in patty form)
- Steaks
- Turkey
- Venison

When freezing raw meat place the portions into mylar bags with oxygen absorbers or follow your preferred method to freeze dry. Raw meat can successfully last for around 10-15 years and by just immersing the product in water for a short period and drying with a paper towel, the meat is then ready as the main ingredient in many exciting recipes that you can create for you and your family.

Dried meat can also safely be freeze-dried by firstly removing any excess fat and checking during the freeze-drying process that crystallized ice cannot be seen inside the meat. If it does, then just increase the drying time until it is gone. Then store in the same way. Always ensure with these products as with all food items that you clearly label the food, what it is, raw or cooked, and the date you freeze-dried it to ensure when rehydrated the food will be at its best.

Dried meat must be rehydrated in cold water overnight in the refrigerator and then cooked as you prefer for your creative dish.

Fish

Fish that can be freeze-dried include:

- Cod
- Pollock
- Haddock
- Mackerel
- Sardines
- Herring
- Tuna
- salmon

These types of fish will preserve longer due to their low-fat content. Rehydration for fish is easy, just by adding water with its flavor and smell returning quickly making it a perfect ingredient for any fish-based dish that's easy and quick to prepare.

Ready prepared meals

Meals that can be freeze-dried include:

- Lasagna
- Pasta dishes (or pasta itself, however, plain pasta is difficult)
- pizzas
- Macaroni and cheese
- Enchiladas
- fajitas
- chili

- Meatballs
- Meatloaf
- Mashed potatoes
- Rice dishes (part boiled rice is better than fully cooked rice)
- Casseroles
- Chicken dishes
- Noodle dishes
- Roast meals
- Stews
- Soups (creamier/fatty soups preserve for around 5-15 years)

Many different meals can be frozen making it particularly useful for families as meals that the whole family enjoys can be prepared and stored for later use. Prepared meals when placed on a tray should be layered no more than half an inch thick for the moisture to be absorbed to aid in the freeze-drying process. If the meal you have prepared is taller than this measurement, you must leave more space around the meal when placing it on the tray or individual portions could be freeze-dried in the freezer before placing into mylar bags with oxygen absorbers, making it easy to rehydrate and cook for one person or the whole family. To reconstitute your prepared meal just add water, heat/cook your preferred way and serve. Some meals may take longer to reconstitute. Tip- avoid adding too much water as this can cause some foods to become soggy.

Desserts

Desserts that can be freeze-dried include:

- Cheesecakes
- Cookies
- Ice cream (using small scoops and pre-freeze the dryer)
- Jell-o (cut into small cubes)
- Pies
- Puddings
- Marshmallows

It is easy to freeze-dry your sweet treats and my particular favorite to store. The main thing to remember when freeze-drying sweet items is to cut them into small pieces and if you are using a freeze dryer then you must pre-set it to cold, so the trays go in cold, to begin with.

Herbs and spices

Herbs and spices that freeze dry include:

* Basil
* Garlic
* Ginger
* Lavender
* Sage
* Thyme
* Oregano
* Mint
* Chives
* Horseradish
* Jalapeno

Spices and herbs freeze dry well due to their delicate nature, but one handy hint to remember if using a freeze dryer is to avoid putting them in with other foods, otherwise, the smells and taste of the spice/herb may contaminate the other item.

Drinks

* Smoothies
* Coffee
* Orange juice

Orange juice and smoothies can easily be freeze-dried. just pour onto a tray, freeze, and transfer to sealed bags with an oxygen absorber. Coffee is perfect for freeze-drying.

Other items

- **Bread**

This can be freeze-dried if sliced but requires reconstitution with humidity or the bread will remain soggy, so not great if you wish to make a sandwich or toast.

- **Condiments**

Watered down and well mixed, condiments such as ketchup, BBQ sauces, and mustard can be freeze-dried.

Some foods either do <u>not freeze dry</u> or may do when contained within another food item. Items in this category include:

- **Alcohol**. When a small amount is in another food then this is possible, but on its own does not freeze dry.
- **Butter**. It can be freeze-dried if an ingredient in another food but will not have a long shelf life.
- **Peanut butter**. Has a high sugar and fat content, so on its own does not freeze-dry well, unless contained in another food source.
- **Honey**. Due to its high sugar content and being thick and sticky, this will not freeze dry. However, it does have a naturally long shelf life.
- **Oily and fatty foods**. These foods over time will have an unpleasant taste and smell and will have a shortened shelf life.
- **Sugary foods.** These require to be checked for moisture before transferring to a storage bag due to their chemical makeup and high sugar content.
- **Chocolate.** Less pure chocolate may freeze-dry if contained in other foods.
- **Thick cream.** Can be watered down and put into ice cube trays but due to its high-fat content will not have a long shelf life.
- **Mayonnaise.** Too high a fat content to freeze-dry. An alternative could be cream cheese.
- **Nuts.** Freeze drying can freshen nuts, however, whole nuts do not freeze-dry well. Again, if a product such as a baked biscuit etc. contains nuts this could be freeze-dried.
- **Nutella.** Due to its high fat, sugar, and nut content, unless as part of another food this will not freeze dry.

- **Preserves, jams, and jellies.** Due to their high sugar content, these will not freeze-dry. However, if you are freeze-drying fruit, these can then be used to make these products.
- **Syrup.** Too thick and sugary to freeze-dry, but they do generally have a long shelf life without the need to freeze-dry.

As discussed, the list of foods that potentially can be freeze-dried to use as ingredients in the preparation of a variety of meals is quite extensive. Now we can look at recipe ideas that you could follow to provide meals for you and your family for the times ahead.

Chapter 5

Recipes

Cooking with freeze-dried products enables fast and easy preparation of meals for yourself and your family. As all the hard work has already been done in terms of prepping your ingredients in terms of washing, cutting, slicing, etc., this enables you to bring the meal together successfully. During the freeze-drying process as moisture is removed from the product when you come to rehydrate the ingredient to be used then it will not contain too much water, in particular when using freeze-dried vegetables in soups. The soup will remain a thicker consistency and therefore improving the texture and taste of your soup.

Also, in preparing ingredients yourself to use in recipes you know exactly what is going into your meal, with no hidden additives or preservatives ensuring your family has a well-balanced nutritional meal. An interesting by-product of the freeze-drying process is that it makes the end product gluten-free making the meal suitable for many dietary requirements.

To follow are just some of the meals, (perhaps ones that could be your family favorites) that can be made and freeze-dried for use in the future and a selection of recipes that can be prepared using freeze-dried ingredients.

The specifics of the freeze-drying methods and how to freeze-dry particular foods along with the rehydration of these products to use in your meal preparation have been discussed earlier. With that said, let's move on to a variety of meals for all to enjoy!

Recipes To Prepare and Freeze-Dry

Recipe ideas that can be prepared in advance and stored for the future by the freeze-drying process, ensuring your family have a selection of meals not only quick to prepare but ones you'll know they will enjoy. These recipes are made using a freeze-dryer and transferred to mylar bags, however other alternative methods to freeze dry the foods could be used. The best thing to do is to choose not only the most practical method to freeze dry your foods but also the most economical method to meet the needs of you and your family.

Strawberry Smoothie

A delicious and healthy start to your day.

Prep time: 5 mins Serves: 1 (just increase quantities if making for 4)

Ingredients:

1. 10 strawberries (hulled)
2. 100mls orange juice
3. 1 sliced small banana

Method:

1. In a blender pulse the ingredients until a smooth consistency is obtained.
2. Pour into a smoothie glass and enjoy!

To freeze- dry:

1. Pour the liquid straight onto your freeze dry tray and follow the manufacturer's recommendations.
2. Transfer the dried flakes to a storage jar for later use
3. When ready to consume just add cold water slowly to achieve the desired consistency.

Blueberry Smoothie

This delicious smoothie is packed full of goodness.

Prep time: 5 mins Serves:2

Ingredients:

1. ½ cup apple juice. Also, could use grape juice/dairy milk or almond milk
2. 1 ½ cups blueberries
3. 1 banana (cut in two)
4. ¾ cup vanilla Greek yogurt
5. Extra blueberries and mint leaves to garnish

Method:

1. In a blender mix the apple juice, Greek yogurt, banana, and blueberries.
2. Blend until smooth
3. Pour into glasses and decorate with the extra blueberries and mint leaves.

To freeze- dry: Follow the method as per the previous recipe.

Banana Smoothie

A creamy fruity delight!

Prep time: 5 mins Serves: 1

Ingredients:

1. 1 banana(chopped)
2. ½ orange (peeled, cut in quarters)
3. 1/3 cup Greek yogurt
4. ¼ cup water or milk
5. 1-2 tsp honey

Method:

1. Add the banana and orange to a blender.
2. Then add the yogurt and water (or milk).
3. Blend until smooth and creamy.
4. Add the honey if required.

To freeze-dry: Follow previous smoothie recipes

Cantaloupe Smoothie

This creamy, yet refreshing smoothie is simply delicious.

Prep time: 5 mins Serves: 1

Ingredients:

1. 2-3 cups cantaloupe(cubed)
2. 1 banana(sliced)
3. ½ cup yogurt
4. 1 cup milk
5. 1-2 cups ice cubes

Method:

1. In a blender add the cantaloupe, banana, milk, yogurt, and ice.
2. Blend until smooth.

To freeze-dry: Follow previous smoothie recipes

Tomato and Basil soup

A favorite soup to enjoy as a starter or with bread as a meal on its own.

Prep time: 10 mins Cook Time: 20 mins Serves: 4-6

Ingredients:

1. 2 fresh basil leaves
2. 1 onion, chopped (medium-sized)
3. 1 bay leaf
4. 2 – 28 oz. cans of drained whole tomatoes
5. 1 cup heavy cream
6. 2 chopped garlic cloves
7. 1 tsp salt
8. ½ tsp pepper

Method:

1. In a pot add the onions, bay leaf, and basil.
2. Allow simmering for around 20 mins.
3. Take out the bay leaf and in a blender puree the mixture.
4. Pour back into the pot.
5. Add salt and pepper.
6. Avoid adding the cream when freeze-drying.
7. Freeze- dry using your chosen method (can be poured onto your trays, freeze-dried, and transferred in small pieces to an airtight jar to store.
8. To rehydrate just add hot water until your chosen consistency is obtained and then add the cream, avoiding boiling the mixture.
9. Serve in bowls to enjoy this tasty soup.

Chicken, Rice and Vegetable Soup

A hearty vegetable soup to satisfy those appetites.

Prep Time: 10 mins Cook Time: 50 mins Serves: 4

Ingredients:

1. ½ cup cooked diced chicken breast
2. ½ cup wild rice
3. ¼ cup spinach
4. ½ cup button mushrooms
5. 1 bay leaf
6. ½ tsp dried basil
7. ½ tsp garlic powder
8. 3 tsp of chicken stock
9. ¼ tsp ground black pepper
10. ¼ tsp iodized sea salt
11. 4 cups water

Method:

1. Place all the ingredients into a medium-sized pot (apart from the basil).
2. Add 4 cups of water.
3. Bring to a boil.
4. Cover and simmer for 45-60 mins (adding the basil at the end of cooking time).
5. Freeze- dry as per the previous recipe to store and rehydrate when needed to. Enjoy!

Turkey Noodle Soup

A warming filling tasty soup

Prep Time: 20 mins Cook Time: 1 hour Serves: 4-6

Ingredients:

1. 24 oz packet of frozen egg noodles (thaw and boil for 20 mins)
2. 2 cartons turkey broth (32 oz each)
3. 2 lbs. cooked turkey
4. 3 cups chopped celery
5. 3 cups chopped carrots
6. 1 cup chopped onion
7. 1 can cream of chicken soup
8. 2 cups heavy cream
9. ½ cube butter
10. 2 packets dry Italian dressing seasoning
11. Salt and pepper to taste

Method:

1. In a large pot add the turkey broth and bring to a boil.
2. Add the cooked noodles, onion, celery, carrots, turkey, and seasoning.
3. Adjust to simmer for 30 mins.
4. Cool down the soup slightly and add the cream of chicken soup and the butter.
5. Stir until the soup is creamy.

To freeze dry:

1. Add the soup mix to your trays and run through the freeze-dryer.
2. Transfer to an airtight mylar bag.
3. When rehydrating add hot water until the soup reaches the thickness that you require and stir in the heavy cream and enjoy.

Lentil Soup

Soup packed full of vegetables, filling and nutritious.

Prep time: 15-20 mins Cook time: 75 mins Serves: 8

Ingredients:

1. 1 onion(chopped)
2. 2 cups dry lentils
3. 2 carrots(diced)
4. 2 celery sticks(chopped)
5. ¼ cup olive oil
6. 2 garlic cloves(minced)
7. 1 bay leaf
8. 1 tsp dried basil
9. 1 tsp dried oregano
10. 1 (14.5 oz) can of tomatoes
11. ½ cup spinach (sliced thin)
12. 8 cups water
13. 2 tbsp vinegar
14. Salt and pepper to taste

Method:

1. In a large soup pot, heat the oil over medium heat.
2. Add the celery, carrots, and onions and cook for 3-5 mins (until the onions are soft).
3. Stir in the basil, oregano, bay leaf, and garlic and cook for 2 minutes.
4. Add the lentils, water, and tomatoes and bring them to a boil.
5. Reduce to simmer for 1 hour (until the lentils are soft).
6. Stir in the spinach to cook, add vinegar, salt, and pepper and serve in bowls. Enjoy!

To freeze-dry:

1. Pour the mixture onto the freeze-dry trays and process.
2. Transfer to mylar bags to store until their use.
3. Add warm water to rehydrate.

Freeze-dried Eggs

A simple recipe to freeze-dry eggs. As an ingredient on its own, it is used in so many recipes and can be used to make many meals.

Prep time: 10 min Cook time: 16 hours Yield: 12

Ingredients:

1. 12 eggs

Method:

1. Beat the eggs and add to a hot pan.
2. Cook fully, turning over after 3 minutes, and cut into circles using a cutter.
3. Once cooked, place the circles on the freeze-drying tray.
4. Follow the specific instructions for your dryer.
5. Remove when done and store in mylar bags.
6. When ready to use, add 2 tablespoons of water with 3 circles of eggs. Stir until rehydrated.
7. To achieve a softer egg, add more water.
8. If you crumble the egg, add 2 tablespoons of egg powder to 2 tablespoons of water to make the equivalent of one egg.

Beef Fajitas

As part of your main meal or a delicious snack, these go down a treat with the whole family.

Prep time: 20 mins Cook time: 10 mins Serves: 6

Ingredients:

1. 6 pcs 5-inch tortillas
2. 2lbs beef strips
3. 1 cup cheddar cheese/Mexican blend
4. 1 red bell pepper (seeds removed and sliced into strips)
5. 1 cup salsa
6. ¼ cup onion(diced)
7. 1 ½ tbsp. taco and fajita spice mix or taco seasoning.
8. ¼ cup water

Method:

1. Warm a pan over medium heat.
2. Add the beef, onion, bell pepper, and seasoning.
3. To prevent the mixture from drying, add the water.
4. For around 8-10 minutes stir fry the ingredients until the pepper is soft and the beef has browned.
5. Add the mixture to the tortillas with a spoonful of salsa and a sprinkling of cheese.

To freeze- dry:

1. The mixture for the tortillas can be laid out on a tray and freeze-dried. The cheese may need a little room above the tray as it may expand slightly.
2. The tortillas can be freeze-dried, however, they just need to be rehydrated in a humid environment or they could end up soggy.

Chicken Pot Pie

Love chicken pies? Then try this chicken pot pie recipe that's tasty and sure to please the entire family and one they can enjoy time and time again.

Prep Time: 30 mins Cook Time:25 mins Servings: 12

Ingredients:

Crust:

1. 2 ½ cups of flour
2. 1 cup cubed butter (chilled)
3. 1 tsp salt
4. 1 tsp sugar
5. 1 cup ice cold water

Filling:

1. 8 cups chopped chicken
2. 2 cups diced onions
3. 2 cups diced celery
4. 2 cups diced carrots
5. 2 cups peas
6. 2 cups heavy cream or half milk/half cream
7. 1 cup flour
8. 4 cups bone chicken broth
9. 2/3 cup butter
10. Salt and pepper to taste

Crust method:

1. In a food processor add the flour, sugar, butter, and salt and pulse until a crumbly consistency is obtained.
2. Whilst running add the ice-cold water until the dough mixture comes together.
3. Remove and knead until a firm ball of dough is formed.
4. Chill for 20 mins divided into 4 parts.

5. Roll out to a ¼ inch thick and cut into small circles of pie crusts.
6. Lay these on a greaseproof baking sheet and cook for 5- 10 mins at 375 degrees F/190 degrees C

Filling method:

1. Over medium heat in a large pan melt 2 tbsp butter.
2. Add in the chicken to cook. Just before it's cooked add the diced vegetables.
3. When the vegetables become soft add the remaining butter to melt.
4. Add flour to the mixture and cookout (3-5 mins)
5. Once the flour has turned golden brown add the cream and broth and stir.
6. Add the peas, pepper, and salt, and stir until the mixture has thickened.
7. Take off the heat and allow it to cool.

To freeze- dry:

1. Fill the trays with the filling mix.
2. Lay the crusts on another tray.
3. When freeze dried break up the filling mixture into storage jars and add one crumbled pie crust and oxygen absorber to the jar, then a two-part canning lid.

To have this meal at a later date, add 1 cup of boiling water to the jar, replace the lid and shake slowly. Once the water has been absorbed it's time to enjoy!

Vegan Mushroom Stew

Packed full of vegetables and lentils ensures this hearty meal is packed full of goodness for the whole family.

Prep time:10 mins Cook time: 35 mins Serves: 6

Ingredients:

1. 3 tbsp olive oil
2. 6 cloves of garlic(sliced)
3. 16 oz. halved baby mushrooms
4. 1 cup carrot(sliced)
5. 1 cup celery (sliced)
6. 1 yellow onion (diced)
7. ½ tsp sage(dried)
8. 2 tsp thyme(dried)
9. 1 tsp oregano(dried)
10. 2 tbsp flour
11. 2 tbsp soy sauce
12. ¼ cup balsamic vinegar
13. 16 oz small yellow potatoes (halved)
14. 1 cup split red lentils
15. 1 can tomato sauce (14.5 oz.)
16. 2 bay leaves
17. 3 cups vegetable broth
18. Kosher salt
19. Fresh pepper

Method:

1. In a large pot over medium heat, heat the oil.
2. Add celery, carrots, onion, salt, and pepper.
3. Cook whilst stirring for 8 mins.
4. Add the sage, mushrooms, thyme, garlic, and oregano, and season with salt and pepper.

5. Stir and cook for 3-4 minutes.
6. Add the flour, stir and cook for a further minute to coat the ingredients in the flour.
7. Add the vinegar and soy sauce to deglaze the pan.
8. Next add the bay leaves, tomato sauce, broth, potatoes, lentils, and season.
9. Over medium heat, simmer gently to ensure the lentils don't get stuck to the pan.
10. Reduce to low heat and simmer for a further 10-15 minutes until the potatoes are soft. Season to taste.
11. Decorate with fresh parsley and enjoy with some mashed potatoes.

Herby Garlic Mashed Potatoes

An ideal dish to have prepared to accompany many meals.

Prep time: 10 minutes Cook time: 7 minutes Serves: 12 ½ cups

Ingredients:

1. 3 lbs. potatoes, peeled and chopped into 1-inch pieces
2. 6 tsp garlic(minced)
3. 4 cups water
4. 1 cup heavy cream
5. 1 tsp white vinegar
6. 3 tbsp butter
7. ¼ cup fresh parsley (chopped)(1 ½ tbsp dried)
8. ¼ cup fresh/ freeze-dried chives
9. 3 tsp kosher salt
10. ½ tsp ground pepper

Instructions:

1. Bring a large pan of water to boil and add the potatoes, garlic, vinegar, and 1 tsp salt.
2. Once the potatoes are soft, remove and drain well.
3. Add the heavy cream and 1-2 tsp salt to the pot and mash the potatoes.
4. Add the parsley, pepper, chives, and butter and mash further until smooth. If required add further salt and pepper.

To Freeze dry:

1. The day before freeze-drying place the mashed potatoes in the fridge.
2. Remove from the fridge and scatter the mash onto the freeze dry trays. Allow room (avoid tightly packing) around the mixture for the process to be most effective.
3. Avoid freeze drying any more than 5 pounds at a time as again will prevent the drying process.
4. If the mixture crumbles easily then it is ready.
5. Store the mash in mylar bags with an oxygen and moisture absorber.
6. To rehydrate heat ¼-1/2 a cup of water per 1 cup of mash.
7. Add the water slowly over the mash and mix until you achieve the consistency that you prefer.

Skillet Mushroom Chicken

A delicious recipe for the family and perfect to freeze-dry.

Prep time: 10 mins Cook time: 10 mins Serves:4

Ingredients:

For the chicken:

1. 1 ½ lb. chicken breasts(boneless)
2. 2 tbsp extra virgin olive oil
3. 1 tsp oregano
4. 1 tsp paprika
5. 1 tsp coriander
6. Salt and pepper to taste

For the sauce:

1. 12 oz. fresh mushrooms(sliced)
2. ½ cup chicken broth
3. 3 green onions(chopped)
4. 2 garlic cloves(minced)
5. 1 tbsp unsalted butter
6. Parsley to garnish
7. Salt and pepper to taste

Method:

1. Heat an oven to 200 degrees F/93 degrees C
2. Cut the chicken breasts in half, dry with a paper towel, and season with salt and pepper.
3. In a bowl mix together the coriander, paprika, and oregano, and season the chicken with this mixture.
4. In a skillet heat the olive oil, add the chicken, and cook for 3-4 minutes on each side.
5. Transfer the chicken to an oven tray and place it in the oven.

6. Using the same skillet add more olive oil, and melt the butter. Sautee the mushrooms for 5 minutes.
7. Add the broth, onions, salt, and pepper and bring to a boil.
8. Remove the chicken from the oven and place it in the skillet and using a spoon baste the chicken with the sauce.
9. Serve, garnish with parsley and enjoy!

To freeze-dry:

1. Divide the final dish into 4 portions and freeze-dry and transfer to mylar bags for storage until you're ready to consume.

Chicken and Onions

An easy recipe to cook and share with your family. Complete the meal by adding vegetables or rice.

Prep time: 10 mins Cook time: 1 hour Serves:8-10

Ingredients:

1. 5 lb. chicken breasts
2. Paprika
3. Garlic powder
4. 2 onions(chopped)
5. 6 garlic cloves(pressed)
6. Olive oil
7. ¼ tsp red pepper flakes
8. 1 tbsp oregano
9. Salt and pepper

Method:

1. Lay the chicken breasts on a greaseproof tray.
2. Sprinkle the breasts with garlic powder, paprika, salt, and pepper.
3. In a pan fry the onions in olive oil. Add the garlic, oregano, and red pepper flakes.
4. Add the mixture to the chicken breasts.
5. Cover and bake for 1 hour.

To freeze- dry:

1. Slice the chicken into strips and place it on the freeze-dry trays to process.
2. To rehydrate, simply add warm water or broth to the chicken and use it in your recipes.

Classic Chili

A delicious take on this family favorite.

Prep Time:5 mins Cook Time:25 mins Serves 6

Ingredients:

1. 1 lb. ground beef (lean)
2. 1 yellow onion (medium, diced)
3. 1 tbsp olive oil
4. 1 tbsp garlic powder
5. 2 ½ tbsp chili powder
6. 1 ½ cups beef broth
7. 1 15 oz can tomato(diced)
8. 1 16 oz can of red kidney beans (rinsed and drained)
9. 8 oz can of tomato sauce
10. 2 tbsp cumin(ground)
11. 2 tbsp tomato paste
12. 2 tbsp sugar(granulated)
13. ¼ tsp ground cayenne pepper
14. 1 ½ tsp salt
15. ½ tsp ground black pepper

Method:

1. In a large pot add the olive oil over medium-high heat for two minutes
2. Add the onion and continue to cook for another 5 mins.
3. Add the ground beef, separate, and cook until browned, around 6 mins.
4. Add the tomato paste, garlic powder, chili powder, cumin, sugar, salt, pepper, and cayenne. Stir until well mixed together.
5. Add the tomatoes, tomato sauce, drained beans, and broth and stir.
6. Bring the liquid to a low boil, then reduce the heat and simmer for 20-25 minutes uncovered. Stir a few times.
7. Take off the heat and leave to rest for 5-10 mins before serving.

To freeze- dry:

1. Pour the chili onto the tray and process.
2. To rehydrate, simply add hot water and stir until you are happy with the consistency.
3. Serve with bread or tortilla chips.

Beef Casserole

Packed full of goodness, this casserole makes for a healthy hearty meal for the family.

Prep time: 10 mins Cook time: 90 mins Serves: 4

Ingredients:

1. 1 ½ lb. of beef steak
2. 1 large onion(chopped)
3. 1 oz corn flour
4. 7 mushrooms(sliced)
5. 3 carrots(sliced)
6. 1-pint beef stock or 2 stock cubes in 575 ml of warm water
7. 1 dessertspoon cooking oil
8. 1 tbsp tomato puree
9. Salt and pepper to taste

Method:

1. Preheat oven to 150 degrees C /325 degrees F.
2. Cut the beef into strips
3. In a pan heat the oil and fry the carrots, mushrooms, and onions for 2-3 mins.
4. Pour into a casserole dish.
5. Fry the beef strips.
6. Add the cooked beef strips to the casserole dish leaving the liquid in the pan.
7. Mix the corn flour with the water and add to the juice in the pan. Cook for 2-3 mins.
8. Stir in the stock and bring it to a boil.
9. Add the tomato puree, salt, and pepper.
10. Add the sauce to the casserole dish and cook for 1 ½ hour.

To freeze dry:

1. Add the finished meal to freeze-dry trays, process, and then divide into equal portions into mylar bags for the family to enjoy another time.

Italian Beef Lasagna

A true family favorite, satisfying and delicious

Prep Time: 15 mins Cook Time: 4 hours Serves: 8-10

Ingredients: Ragu

1. 1 lb. minced ground beef
2. 1 lb. minced ground pork
3. 1 tbsp olive oil
4. 2 ½ cups passata (sieved tomatoes).
5. 3 tbsp tomato paste
6. 1 cup red wine(250ml)
7. 6 cups beef stock
8. 1 cup finely chopped white onion.
9. 1 cup chopped celery stalks
10. 1 cup finely chopped carrot
11. 2 bay leaves
12. 1 tsp sea salt
13. 1 tsp pepper

Ingredients: White sauce

1. 5 tbsp flour
2. 1 cup grated parmesan
3. 5 tbsp butter
4. 4 cups of full-fat milk
5. ½ tsp nutmeg
6. 1 tsp sea salt and pepper to taste

Ingredients: Lasagna

1. 1 lb. lasagna pasta sheets
2. 2 balls of mozzarella (8 oz.)

Instructions: Ragu

1. Sauté the vegetables in the frying pan with olive oil.
2. When they are soft add the beef and pork to brown.
3. Expel any surplus fat and add red wine to reduce it.
4. Then add the tomatoes, paste, 4 cups of beef stock, salt, and pepper.
5. Simmer uncovered for 2.5-3 hours, adding the remaining beef stock halfway.

Instructions: White sauce

1. Melt the butter in a saucepan.
2. Add the flour and mix to form a paste and cook for 1 minute.
3. Whisk in half the butter and flour. Once thickened, add the remaining milk, parmesan, nutmeg, salt, and pepper to taste.
4. Stir the sauce until thickened. Remove from heat and put to one side.

Assemble the lasagna:

1. On the base of the dish add a layer of ragu, then a layer of pasta sheets.
2. Add more spoons of ragu covering the pasta, then cover with the white sauce.
3. Continue layering until all of the mixture is used, leaving some white sauce for the topping.
4. Pull apart the mozzarella and cover the top.

To freeze- dry:

1. Divide into individual portions and freeze-dry
2. Place in mylar bags with an oxygen absorber.
3. To cook, remove portions from the bags, add water to rehydrate, and transfer to a baking dish.
4. Cook in the oven at 350 degrees F (180 C) for 45 minutes.
5. Allow to cool for 5-10 minutes then serve, Enjoy!

Spaghetti Bolognese

A highly popular dish loved by many.

Prep time: 10 min Cook time: 1 hour Serves: 5

Ingredients:

1. 1 diced onion
2. 1 diced carrot
3. 1 celery stick(diced)
4. 2 minced garlic cloves
5. 2 tbsp olive oil
6. ½ lb. Lean beef, (ground)
7. 6 oz. Italian sausage(ground)
8. 18 oz can tomatoes(chopped)
9. 1 cup red wine
10. 12 oz spaghetti
11. 1 tsp fresh sage
12. 1 tsp fresh rosemary
13. Salt and pepper to taste
14. Parmesan cheese to garnish
15. Parsley to garnish.

Method:

1. In a large saucepan heat the olive oil.
2. Add the celery, carrots, and onions and cook until they are soft. (5 mins).
3. Add the beef and sausage, browning for around 7-10 mins. Finally, add the garlic.
4. Use the wine to make a sauce in the pan.
5. Add the seasonings and the tomatoes and simmer for an hour.
6. Add salt and pepper to taste.
7. Cook and drain the spaghetti, then add it to the pasta sauce.
8. Decorate with parmesan and parsley to serve.

To freeze- dry:

1. Once the spaghetti is cooked, keep separate from the meat sauce to freeze dry on trays.
2. Add water to the meat sauce to rehydrate and mix in the noodles to serve.

Margherita Pizza

Great for a snack or as part of a meal, this pizza is sure to appeal to all tastes.

Prep time: 25 mins Cook time: 10 mins Serves: 4(2 pizzas)

Ingredients:

Base:

1. 300 g strong bread flour
2. 1 tbsp olive oil
3. 1 tsp instant yeast
4. 1 tsp salt

Tomato sauce:

1. 100 ml passata
2. 1 crushed garlic clove
3. 1 tsp dried basil

Topping:

1. 125g mozzarella sliced
2. Parmesan cheese (or veg option)
3. Cherry tomatoes (cut in half)

Finish:

1. Basil to top

Method: Base

1. In a large bowl add the flour, yeast, and salt.
2. Add 200mls of warm water and olive oil and mix until a soft dough is achieved.
3. Knead on a floured service for 5 minutes. Set to one side, covered to rise.

Sauce:

1. Add together the passata, garlic, and basil and set to one side.

Base:

1. Knead, divide into two equal balls, and roll out into 2 x 25cm round bases.
2. Transfer to two floured baking sheets.

Bake:

1. Preheat oven to 260 degrees F/130 degrees C
2. Spread the sauce over the bases. Add the cheese, tomatoes, and olive oil.
3. Bake in the oven for 8-10 minutes.
4. Transfer to a pizza board and drizzle a little olive oil on top with basil leaves.

To freeze dry:

1. Cut up the pizza into slices and lay it on your freeze-dry tray.
2. Once freeze-dried, to rehydrate for consumption, spray with water or cover with paper towels.

Cheesy Macaroni

A tasty recipe that's great for lunch or an evening meal.

Prep Time:15 mins Cook Time: 20 mins Serves: 8

Ingredients:

1. 16 oz. Pasta (raw)
2. 2 ¾ cups milk
3. ¼ cup all-purpose flour
4. 1 cup smoked gouda cheese(shredded)
5. 1 cup cheddar cheese(shredded)
6. ½ cup cheddar cheese powder
7. ½ tsp mustard powder
8. ½ tsp smoked paprika
9. ½ tsp black pepper
10. ½ tsp salt to taste

Method:

1. In salted boiling water cook the pasta and leave to one side.
2. In a large pan add the flour, cheese powder, and milk, and bring to a boil.
3. Take off the heat and add the cheese and seasonings. Stir until the cheese has melted.
4. Add the pasta to the cheese mixture.

To freeze dry:

1. Pour the mixture onto the trays and pre-freeze.
2. Using the non-liquid setting freeze dry the meal.
3. When done, add the mixture to a mylar bag with an oxygen absorber.

To enjoy this meal later take out the oxygen absorber from the bag and add hot water. Fold the bag's top and leave for 10 mins, stirring halfway. Then transfer to your dish and tuck in!

Alfredo Pasta with Asparagus

A delicious pasta packed full of goodness and full of flavor.

Prep time: 10 mins Cook time: 20 mins Serves:2

Ingredients:

1. 8 oz alfredo pasta
2. ¾ cup cashew nuts (cut in half)
3. 1 tbsp avocado oil
4. 1 garlic clove
5. 1 tbsp lemon juice
6. 2 tsp nutritional yeast
7. ½ tsp pepper
8. ½ tsp salt
9. 1 bunch of asparagus
10. 1/8 tsp nutmeg
11. ¼ cup parsley(chopped)

Method:

1. Place the cashews in a jar, cover with water, close the lid and leave overnight.
2. Following day, drain and rinse the cashews. Put them in a blender with ½ cup water, garlic, lemon juice, yeast, nutmeg, pepper, and salt. Blend until a smooth mixture is obtained.
3. Cut the ends off the asparagus and cut them into 2-inch lengths. Sprinkle them with avocado oil, salt, and pepper, and grill them.
4. Add the pasta to a large pot of boiling water. Mix the pasta with the sauce and the asparagus and transfer to serving bowls. Sprinkle parmesan on top to complete this tasty dish.

To freeze- dry:

1. When cooking the pasta if you are freeze-drying it to store, then only partially cook the pasta (al dente) so when it rehydrates it doesn't become all soggy and stick together.
2. The rest of the recipe can be freeze-dried and transferred to mylar bags.

Barbecued Turkey Meatballs

Delicious meatballs to enjoy with rice or pasta dishes, a tasty meal for the whole family.

Prep Time: 30 mins Cook Time: 15-20 mins Serves: 3-4

Ingredients:

1. 1 lb. ground turkey
2. 1 cup whole wheat bread crumbs
3. 1 garlic clove (minced)
4. ¼ cup parmesan cheese(grated)
5. 1 egg(beaten)
6. ¼ cup onion(minced)
7. 2 tsp fresh thyme
8. ½ tsp black pepper
9. ½ tsp salt

Method:

1. Mix all the ingredients and form 2" meatballs.
2. On a baking sheet broil for 10 mins.

Ingredients for the sauce:

1. 1 tbsp soy sauce.
2. 1 tbsp coconut oil
3. 3 garlic cloves(minced)
4. 1 small onion(diced)
5. 1 tsp mustard powder
6. 1 tsp chili powder
7. 1 tsp cumin
8. 1 tsp oregano
9. 2 cups chicken stock
10. 6 oz tomato paste
11. 2 tbsp apple cider vinegar
12. 1 tsp stevia

Method:

1. Cook the onion and garlic in the coconut oil, then add the rest of the ingredients
2. Simmer until a thick sauce is obtained.

To freeze- dry:

1. Arrange the meatballs on the freeze-dry tray/trays
2. Set to a standard setting to freeze dry.
3. Transfer to an airtight container
4. To rehydrate, add hot water slowly in a covered dish or in a microwave until all the water is absorbed.

Pork and Broccoli Stir Fry

A tasty stir fry to prepare for your family when craving a touch of the orient.

Prep time: 10 mins Cook time: 10 mins Serves:4

Ingredients:

For the stir fry:

1. 500 g sliced pork tenderloin
2. 300 g Tenderstem broccoli
3. 2 tbsp sesame oil
4. 3 nests of egg noodles

For the sauce:

1. 3 tbsp Shaoxing wine
2. 3 tbsp sesame oil
3. 1 tbsp honey
4. 2 tbsp light soy sauce
5. 1 tbsp oyster sauce
6. 3 garlic cloves
7. 6cm ginger piece (peeled and grated)

Method:

1. In a pot mix all the sauce ingredients and bring to a boil. Simmer and reduce to a consistency to use for coating.
2. In a wok fry the broccoli in the sesame oil until soft but with bite and remove to a plate.
3. Add the pork to the wok and fry for 2 mins, then add the broccoli and the sauce. Toss everything to cover in the sauce.
4. Cook the egg noodles, add to the mixture, and serve.

To freeze- dry:

When freeze drying undercook the noodles so they don't become soggy when re-hydrated. After freeze-drying on a tray bag the meal and store it. When using add water to rehydrate and toss in a wok to warm and finish the noodles.

Salmon and Pesto

A quick and easy meal to prepare for the freeze dryer and rehydrates in no time. A very healthy dish for lunch or evening meal when accompanied with vegetables or rice.

Prep time:5 mins Cook time:5 mins Freeze dry time: as per manufacturers recommendations Serves:4

Ingredients:

1. 4 salmon fillets
2. 1 cup pesto sauce

Method:

1. Broil or bake the salmon for a few minutes until cooked
2. Add a spoonful of pesto to the top of each one.

To freeze-dry:

1. Line the freeze-dry trays with paper towels to help soak up any excess oil from the fillets.
2. Lay the fillets on the tray evenly spaced and process as per your machine's instructions.
3. Check to see that all moisture has been removed from the fillet's centers.
4. Store the fillets in a mylar bag with an oxygen absorber, labeling them with the date you freeze-dried them.
5. To rehydrate, add some hot water slowly until the fish returns to its usual consistency.
6. Rice and vegetables could be added to the fish to make it a complete meal.

Fish Casserole

A filling, and tasty meal when accompanied by bread or vegetables.

Prep time: 5 min Bake time:35 mins Servings: 4

Ingredients:

1. 1 pound cod
2. 1 ½ cups fish broth
3. 3 cups broccoli(chopped)
4. ½ cup long grain rice
5. ¼ tsp garlic powder
6. ¼ tsp Italian seasoning
7. 1 tbsp parmesan cheese(grated)
8. ½ cup cheddar cheese shredded
9. 1 can (28 ounces) of fried onions
10. Pinch of paprika

Method:

1. Add together the broth, seasoning, garlic powder, and rice in a pan and bring to a boil. Transfer to an 11x7 in greased baking dish.
2. Cover and bake for 10 mins at 375 degrees.F/190 degrees C
3. Add the parmesan cheese, the broccoli, and half of the onions.
4. Finish off with the cod fillets and a little paprika.
5. Bake covered for 20-25 mins or until the fish is flaky. Removing the cover add the cheddar cheese and the onions. Pop back into the oven for 2-3 mins for the cheese to melt.

To freeze- dry:

1. Prior freeze drying divide the casserole into separate portions.
2. Freeze- dry and place in mylar bags for future use.

Pumpkin Pie

Enjoy this delicious pie to have on thanksgiving or whenever your family fancies a slice of this tasty pie.

Prep time: 15 mins Cook time: 50 mins Serves: 8

Ingredients:

1. 1 can pumpkin
2. 1 can evaporated milk
3. 2 large eggs
4. ¾ cup sugar
5. ¼ tsp cloves(ground)
6. 1 tsp cinnamon(ground)
7. ½ tsp ginger(ground)
8. ½ tsp salt

Method:

1. Add all the dry ingredients together, and put them on one side.
2. In a large bowl beat the eggs, and add the pumpkin, sugar, and spice mixture.
3. Slowly add in the evaporated milk.
4. Spread the mixture onto your freeze-dry tray.
5. Weigh and make a note of the weight of the wet mixture.
6. Freeze dry and then record the dry weight and take this figure away from the wet weight.
7. Add the freeze-dried mixture to a blender until a powder is formed.
8. Transfer to a mylar bag with an oxygen absorber and record the water weight that will be required to reconstitute the pie mixture.
9. When reconstituted in a blender for around10-15 seconds, pour this mixture into a 9-inch pie base.
10. Heat an oven to 425 degrees F/220 degrees C for 15 mins and then lower it to 350 degrees F/180 degrees C and cook for 40-50 minutes.
11. Check if a knife comes out clean when removed from the center of the pie.
12. Allow to cool for an hour and then serve. Delicious!

Apricot and Apple Crumble

A delicious pudding to complete any meal.

Prep time: 20 mins Cook time: 30 mins Serves: 8

Ingredients:

Filling:

1. 4 apples cut into wedges
2. 825 g can of apricots (drained and the liquid kept to one side)
3. ¼ tsp ground cinnamon
4. Vanilla custard

Crumble:

1. 3-4 cups of plain flour.
2. ½ cup rolled oats
3. ½ cup brown sugar
4. 100 g butter(chilled/sliced)

Method:

1. Preheat oven to 350 degrees F/ 180 degrees C.
2. In a bowl mix together the cinnamon, apricots, and 2/3 cup of the liquid.
3. In a large bowl add the flour, and rub in the butter until breadcrumbs are achieved.
4. Then add the sugar and oats and mix well.
5. Transfer the filling to a large baking dish, sprinkle over the crumble, and bake for 25-30 minutes, checking that the apples are soft.
6. Divide into portions in bowls to enjoy!

To freeze- dry:

1. Add the crumble to a freeze-dry tray, and follow the guidelines. Once freeze-dried divide into portions and store in separate mylar bags for future use.
2. To rehydrate just add water and serve with warm custard. Yum!

Plum Nibbles

A tasty healthy snack, ready when you are.

Prep time: 12 hours Freeze time: 20 hours

Ingredients:

1. 2 lbs. plums
2. ¼ cup honey

Method:

1. Wash the plums and remove the pits, cutting them in half.
2. Place the plums along with the honey in a food processor and blend until a soup consistency is achieved.
3. Pour this mixture into ice cube trays, just below the fill line. Transfer to the freezer until firm.
4. Using parchment paper line freeze- dry trays. With a gap in between each one, lay the ice cubes on the lined trays. Set on a standard cycle.
5. When finished check the cubes have dried right through, they should not be chewy or feel cold to the touch.
6. To store these for a long period transfer them to an airtight container with an oxygen absorber. Keep at room temperature and not in direct sunlight.

Cheesecake

A tasty treat for the family

Prep time: 12 mins Bake time: 30 mins Serves: 6-8

Ingredients:

Crust:

1. ¼ cup confectioners' sugar
2. 1 ½ cups graham cracker crumbs,
3. 5 1/3 tbsp melted butter
4. 1/8 tsp salt

Filling:

1. Two 8-oz packets of cream cheese (room temperature)
2. 2 large eggs
3. 2/3 cup granulated sugar
4. 1 tsp pure vanilla extract

Method:

1. Pre-heat oven to 350 degrees F/180 degrees C and locate a 9" tin
2. To make the crust: mix all the crust ingredients.
3. Press the crumbs into the bottom and up the sides, ensuring it's thicker on the bottom.
4. To make the filling: mix the sugar and cream cheese until smooth.
5. Add the eggs and the vanilla, and mix until smooth. Using an electric mixer blend well the ingredients. If the cream cheese is soft and at room temperature, this should help to avoid lumps in your mixture.
6. Bake for 20 mins, then cover the crust and bake for another 10 mins.
7. Remove from the oven and place on a wire rack to cool.
8. Can be served on its own or with some fresh fruit.

To freeze-dry: Cut the cake into portions to freeze-dry

Chapter 6

Recipes Using Freeze-Dried Foods

Recipe ideas that can be made using freeze-dried ingredients.

Minty Raspberry Surprise Smoothie

A deliciously refreshing smoothie perfect for the start of the day.

Ingredients:

1. ½ cup of water
2. 1 cup of ice
3. ½ cup Greek yogurt- plain (freeze-dried equivalent can be used)
4. 1 freeze-dried banana
5. 1 ¼ cups of freeze-dried raspberries
6. 3 freeze-dried mint leaves (set aside earlier to soften)

Method:

1. Place all the ingredients apart from the ice and mint into a blender and thoroughly mix them.
2. Add the ice and blend
3. Pour into a smoothie glass and garnish with the mint

Body Boost Smoothie

Boost your immune system with this health-conscious smoothie.

Prep time: 10 minutes Serves:1

Ingredients:

1. 2 oranges (or freeze-dried slices)
2. 18g of freeze-dried strawberries
3. 1 tsp powdered ginger
4. 2 tbsp lemon juice
5. 1-2 tsp of honey
6. 50-100mls coconut water (depending on how thick you like your smoothie)
7. 3-5 ice cubes

Method:

1. Place all the ingredients into a blender and blend until the desired texture is achieved.
2. Pour into your favorite smoothie glass and enjoy the boost!

Energizing Tropical Greens Smoothie

When your energy levels are low, how about this great vegetable smoothie pick me up?

Prep time: 10 mins Serves: 1

Ingredients:

1. 18g freeze-dried broccoli
2. 1 cup kale (or freeze-dried quantity)
3. ½ cup pineapple (or freeze-dried quantity)
4. 1 cup coconut water
5. 2 tsp lemon juice

Method:

1. Add all the ingredients into your blender and set too high for 30 seconds or until the desired consistency is achieved.
2. Pour contents into a smoothie glass, drink and feel like a new you!

Berry Good Banana Smoothie

Full of vitamins this healthy smoothie is very tasty, easy to prepare, and a firm favorite of kids and adults alike.

Prep Time:10 mins Serves:1

Ingredients:

1. 2 cups of freeze-dried strawberries
2. 1 cup of Greek yogurt (or freeze-dried equivalent)
3. 2 freeze-dried bananas
4. 2 tbsp of maple syrup
5. 1 cup of ice

Method:

1. Add all the ingredients to a blender, set to high, and pulse for around 45 seconds or until you have achieved a lovely smooth pink drink.
2. Pour into your smoothie glass and decorate with extra freeze-dried strawberries, delicious!

Freeze-Dried Guacamole Recipe

Serving Size:4-6 Servings

Time:5 minutes

Ingredients:

- 3 cups freeze-dried avocados (spritz with lime juice before freeze-drying)
- ½ cup freeze-dried green onions
- ¼ cup freeze-dried cilantro
- 1 cup freeze-dried tomatoes
- 2-4 cloves of freeze-dried garlic
- Freeze-dried bell or hot peppers to taste
- 1/2 teaspoon salt

Directions:

1. Pulse ingredients in a blender until desired size and texture.
2. Pour the contents of the blender into a bowl, stir in 1 cup of water and mix with a fork until guacamole is desired consistency. Add more water 1 teaspoon at a time if needed.
3. Let rest for 1-2 minutes to allow ingredients to absorb moisture.
4. Serve immediately.

Spicy Beetroot Hummus

A tasty dip enjoyed with pitta bread, bread sticks, carrot sticks, etc.

Prep time: 15 mins Serves: 4

Ingredients:

1. 400 g tin chickpeas
2. 1 tbsp extra virgin olive oil
3. 1 small garlic clove
4. 2 tbsp tahini
5. 1 tbsp Lemon juice
6. 1 tsp cumin powder
7. ½ tsp smoked paprika
8. ½ tsp coriander powder
9. 1 tbsp freeze-dried beetroot powder
10. Salt and pepper to taste

Ingredients:

1. Drain the chickpeas and pour them into a blender with all the other ingredients.
2. Blend until a smooth mixture is obtained. Add a little water if the mixture adheres to the sides and blend again.
3. Add salt and pepper to taste and more lemon juice if required.
4. Serve along with your pita bread or crudites.

Beefy Peppered Soup

A warming soup, great for those chilly nights.

Serving size: 1 serving Prep Time: 70 mins Cook time:45 mins

Ingredients:

1. ½ cup white rice
2. 2 cups ground beef
3. ¼ cup dehydrated onion
4. ½ cup freeze-dried bell pepper
5. 1 tsp dehydrated garlic
6. ½ cup tomato sauce
7. Salt and pepper to season

Method:

1. Pour 2 cups of boiling water into a bowl and add the onion and bell peppers. Remove them from the bowl after 15 mins, squeeze out any excess water, and pat dry with a paper towel.
2. Place the beef in a cooking pot on high heat and brown. Will take around 5 minutes.
3. Add the onion/ bell peppers along with the remaining ingredients to the pot, with a cup of water. Cover and simmer for around 40 minutes. Season to taste and serve warm.

Freeze-Dried Noodle & Vegetable Soup

A tasty filling soup packed full of goodness and yet simple to prepare.

Serving Size: 1 serving Cook time: 10-15 minutes

Ingredients:

1. 1 cup of dried noodles
2. 1 cup freeze-dried vegetables (broccoli, green beans, and carrots)
3. ½ tsp onion powder
4. ½ tsp parsley
5. ½ tsp basil
6. ½ tsp garlic powder
7. 4 cups water
8. Salt and pepper to taste

Method:

1. Into a blender add the freeze-dried vegetables and blend into flakes.
2. Set ½ cup to one side.
3. Add 4 cups of water to a pan and bring to a boil.
4. Add the spices and salt.
5. Place the pasta in the pan and once cooked, stir in the freeze-dried vegetables.
6. Simmer for 5 minutes.

Serve hot and enjoy this delicious soup. This recipe could be adjusted for 4 people by multiplying the ingredients by 4.

Tasty Taco Soup

A flavorsome soup. Add some tacos and olives for a filling meal on its own.

Serving size: 4-5 servings Prep time: 20 mins Cook time: 15 min

Ingredients:

1. 1 ½ tsp taco seasoning mix
2. ½ cup freeze-dried ground beef
3. ½ cup black beans
4. 1 ½ cups freeze-dried sweetcorn
5. ¼ cup freeze-dried red and green bell peppers
6. ¼ cup freeze-dried diced tomato
7. ¾ cup freeze-dried green chilies
8. ¼ cup freeze-dried onions, chopped
9. 1 cup freeze-dried tomato powder
10. ¼ cup freeze-dried mix of cheeses (for topping)
11. ¼ cup freeze-dried sour cream (for topping)

Method:

1. Add all the above ingredients to a cooking pot, apart from the cheese and the sour cream.
2. Add 3 cups of water and simmer for around 15 minutes. If the beans are not soft then add a few more minutes.
3. If you require to make a single serving then first add all the ingredients together and divide into four equal portions, then add 1 cup of hot water and microwave for 3-5 minutes, then cover and leave for 5 minutes before serving. Or put in a pot and simmer for around 5-7 minutes, again until the beans are soft.
4. Before serving add the cheese, sour cream, some avocado sliced, and olives.
5. Serve hot and enjoy this delicious soup packed full of goodness.

Tomato and Veggie Surprise Soup

A classic soup packed full of wholesome vegetables that will deliver your family a hearty warming meal.

Prep time: 5 mins Cook time: 15 mins Serves: 4

Ingredients:

1. 4 tsp tomato powder
2. 1 tsp chicken Bouillon (can be left out if vegetarian)
3. ¼ cup freeze-dried peas
4. ¼ cup freeze-dried green beans
5. ½ cup freeze-dried diced potato
6. ¼ cup freeze-dried celery
7. ½ cup freeze-dried sweetcorn
8. ¼ cup freeze-dried sliced onions
9. ¼ cup freeze-dried diced carrots

Method:

1. Put all the ingredients into a large cooking pot.
2. Over medium heat, bring to a boil.
3. Cover with a lid and simmer for 10 minutes and occasionally stir.
4. Serve warm and enjoy this nutritious soup.

Cheese and Spinach Omelette

A quick and easy recipe for breakfast or add vegetables for a filling lunch.

Prep time: 5 mins Cook time: 5 mins Serves: 1

Ingredients:

1. 6 tbsp freeze-dried scrambled egg mix
2. 4 tbsp water
3. 1 tbsp olive oil
4. ½ cup freeze-dried spinach
5. 1 pinch of ground nutmeg
6. ½ cup cheddar cheese(grated)
7. Salt and pepper to taste

Method:

1. Ina bowl mix together the egg mix, salt, pepper, and water.
2. In a frying pan add the oil and the egg mixture.
3. Add the spinach and sprinkle with nutmeg.
4. When nearly cooked sprinkle over the cheese and fold the omelette in half.
5. Transfer to your plate to enjoy on its own or serve with extra vegetables.

Cornbread Muffins

A tasty side to any meal

Prep time:10 mins Cook time: 20 mins

Ingredients:

1. ½ cup freeze-dried corn
2. 1 cup corn meal
3. ½ cup all-purpose flour
4. 1 ½ tsp baking powder
5. 2 tbsp sugar
6. 1 large egg
7. 1 tsp salt
8. 1 ¼ cup buttermilk
9. 2 tbsp unsalted butter

Method:

1. Preheat the oven to 400 degrees F/ 210 degrees C and grease a muffin tray.
2. In a large bowl combine all the dry ingredients.
3. In another bowl, mix the buttermilk and egg.
4. Combine the dry and wet ingredients and mix.
5. Spoon the mixture into the prepared muffin cups.
6. Bake in the oven for 20 mins (or until a knife inserted into a muffin comes out clean).
7. Serve and enjoy these on their own or with your main meal.

Fried Rice

A delicious dish on its own or accompaniment to many dishes.

Prep time: 1 minute Cook time: 12 minutes Serves: 2

Ingredients:

1. 1 vegetable bouillon cube
2. ¼ cup of freeze-dried egg
3. ½ tsp of garlic powder
4. ½ tsp ground ginger
5. ½ tsp brown sugar
6. 1 cup mixed freeze-dried vegetables
7. ¼ tsp salt
8. 2 soy sauce sachets

Method:

1. In a cooking pot with 3 oz. water stir in the egg. Over low heat stir the egg mixture to prevent sticking to the base of the pot. Once cooked remove from the heat and put to one side.
2. In another pot add the vegetables with 1 ¼ cups of water along with the spices. Bring this to a boil, then simmer for around 5 minutes until the vegetables soften.
3. Stir in the rice and move to one side, cover and leave to rest for 5 minutes.
4. Add the egg mixture and stir, warming up the egg mixture.
5. Serve and enjoy or use to accompany a meat or fish dish.

Curried Shrimp Rice

A tasty flavorful rice combining shrimp packed with Indian spices.

Prep time: 30 mins Servings: 1-2

Ingredients:

1. ½ cup freeze-dried shrimp
2. 1 cup rice
3. 1 Tbsp dried onions(diced)
4. 2 Tbsp freeze-dried apples
5. 2 Tbsp raisins
6. 1 tsp curry powder-mild
7. 1/8 tsp ground cinnamon
8. 1/8 tsp ground allspice
9. 1/8 tsp fine sea salt
10. 1 Tbsp olive oil
11. 2 Tbsp cashews(optional)
12. 1 pkt sweet chili sauce

Method:

1. In a pot add 1 ½ cups of water and bring to a boil.
2. Add in the dry ingredients, stir and cover.
3. Remove from the heat and set aside for 15 minutes.
4. Stir in the nuts (if you wish)
5. Add the chili sauce and enjoy!

Pasta Primavera

A delicious Italian classic

Prep time:30-40 mins Serves:4

Ingredients:

1. 1lb wide noodles
2. 1 tsp parsley
3. 2 tsp garlic salt
4. 3 tbsp powdered butter-reconstitute
5. 1 cup freeze-dried broccoli- reconstitute
6. 1 cup freeze-dried carrots
7. 1 cup freeze-dried peas
8. Parmesan cheese
9. Black pepper

Method:

1. Bring a pot of water to a boil and add the noodles. Cook for around 8-10 minutes until al dente.
2. Drain the noodles and place them back into the pot.
3. Add the butter, garlic salt, and parsley to the pot and toss the noodles in this mixture.
4. Stir in the broccoli, carrots, and peas and heat on low until the vegetables are cooked through.
5. According to your taste add parmesan and black pepper.

Tip: to add extra protein to this dish you could add freeze-dried cooked chicken to this meal. Ensure it is reconstituted by adding cold water for a few minutes and then cooking as you would normally and adding to your pasta dish. Enjoy!

Chicken and Mushroom Pasta

A quick and tasty pasta dish to prepare.

Prep time: 20 mins Serves: 2

Ingredients:

1. ½ cup pasta
2. 1 cup freeze-dried chicken
3. ½ cup freeze-dried mushrooms
4. 2 tbsp diced dried onions
5. ½ cup parmesan cheese
6. 1 tbsp freeze-dried garlic
7. 1 tbsp freeze-dried parsley
8. 1/8 tsp sea salt(fine)
9. 2 tbsp olive oil

Method:

1. Add ½ cup of cool water to the chicken and put to one side to reconstitute.
2. Bring 4 cups of water to a boil. Add the pasta, bring it back to the boil, then reduce it to a simmer to cook the pasta.
3. Add in the mushrooms, onions, garlic, parsley, and salt.
4. Add the rehydrated chicken to the pot at the last minute of cooking.
5. Drain off any water left in the pot.
6. Stir in the parmesan cheese and the oil. Serve in a bowl. Delicious.

Chicken Enchiladas

Easy to prepare and enjoy with the family

Prep time: 30 mins Cook time: 25-30 mins Serves 3-4

Ingredients:

1. 1 ½ cups freeze-dried chicken (rehydrated)
2. ¼ cup dehydrated onions
3. 1 ½ cups freeze-dried cheddar cheese
4. 2 cups enchilada sauce
5. 1 cup sour cream
6. Green chiles
7. 6-9 whole wheat tortillas

Directions:

1. Preheat an oven to 375 degrees F/190 degrees C
2. Place the chicken, onions, 1 ½ cups of enchilada sauce, and 1 cup of cheese into a mixing bowl and combine.
3. In a 13 x 9-inch pan pull apart a tortilla to cover the base of the pan.
4. Spread a layer of the mix onto this tortilla.
5. In the pan alternate layers of the mix with layers of tortillas.
6. Finish the top with a tortilla layer and cover with the remaining ½ cup of enchilada sauce.
7. Using the remaining ½ cup of cheese sprinkle over the top
8. Place in the preheated oven for around 25-30 minutes. Serve and enjoy!

Beef and Bean Stew

A hearty beefy vegetable stew to satisfy your hungry family.

Prep time: 10 mins Cook time: 20 mins Serves: 4

Ingredients:

1. 1 cup black beans (quick cook variety)
2. 1 cup freeze-dried beef(diced)
3. 2 tbsp beef bouillon(powdered)
4. 2 tbsp dried minced onions
5. 1 tsp dried garlic
6. 1 cup freeze-dried mixed vegetables
7. 1 cup dried potatoes(diced)
8. 2 tbsp tomato powder
9. 1 tsp thyme
10. 1 tsp salt

Method:

1. Add all the ingredients to a large cooking pot.
2. Add 6 cups of water and bring it up to a boil on medium heat.
3. Reduce the heat and simmer for 20 minutes.
4. Ladle to bowls and enjoy!

Stir-fried Chicken & Broccoli

Enjoy this balanced protein/ veggie mix.

Prep time: 40 mins Cook time: 35-40 mins Serves:1-2

Ingredients:

1. 1 cup freeze-dried chicken
2. 1 cup freeze-dried broccoli
3. ¼ cup carrots
4. 2 tbsp freeze-dried chopped onions
5. ½ cup freeze-dried green peppers
6. 1 cup freeze-dried rice
7. 1/3 cup stir-fried sauce mix

Seasoning mix:

1. ¼ cup chicken bouillon
2. 2 tbsp sugar
3. 3 tbsp corn starch
4. 2 tbsp minced dried onion
5. 2 tsp dried parsley
6. ½ tsp ground ginger
7. ¼ tsp dried red pepper flakes

Method for sauce mix:

1. Mix all the seasoning mix components together.
2. Use 1/3 cup of this mix with 1 ¼ cups of water.
3. Add to a saucepan and using low heat stir until thickens.

Method for meal:

1. Bring 4 cups of water to a boil in a pan.
2. Add all the initial ingredients with the sauce mix and leave to rest for 10 mins.
3. Then cover and simmer for 20-25 minutes.
4. Add the sauce mix to the meal and serve.

Tip: To make more sauce, use 1/3 cup of the sauce mix, add 1 ¼ cups of water, mix and simmer until thickens. Add this to the final dish before serving.

Cheese Chili

A quick and easy cheesy, chili combination

Prep Time: 20-30 mins Serves: 6

Ingredients:

1. ½ cup freeze-dried beef
2. 2 ½ cups macaroni
3. 2/3 cup cheese powder
4. 3 tbsp dry milk
5. 1 ½ tbsp powdered butter
6. ¼ cup taco seasoning mix
7. ½ cup vegetable powder
8. ½ tsp salt
9. ¼ tsp white pepper
10. 2 ½ cups water
11. 3 cups water

Method:

1. To rehydrate the protein and pasta add 3 cups of warm water.
2. Prepare the sauce whilst the pasta is soaking.
3. To the dry ingredients add 2 ½ cups of water, mix and allow to rehydrate.
4. When both parts are rehydrated mix together to serve to enjoy this tasty meal.

Red Curried Chicken with Peanut Coconut Sauce

A deliciously creamy, flavorsome meal.

Prep Time: 10 mins Cook Time: 5-10 mins Serves: 1 (multiply to re-create for additional people)

Ingredients:

1. ¼ cup freeze-dried chicken
2. ½ cup rice
3. ¼ cup dried vegetables
4. 2 tbsp Thai red curry powder
5. 3 tbsp powdered coconut milk
6. 1 tbsp powdered peanut butter
7. 1 tbsp peanuts-chopped
8. ½ pkt freeze-dried lime juice
9. 1 tbsp oil
10. ½ tsp salt

Method:

1. Bring ¾ cup of water to boil in a pan and add all the ingredients.
2. Cover and simmer for 5 mins or until all the ingredients are rehydrated.
3. Serve and enjoy.

Fish Crumble

A cheesy, fishy crumbly delight.

Prep Time:10 mins Cook time: 20 mins Serves:2

Ingredients:

1. 1 freeze-dried boneless pink salmon (rehydrated)
2. 3 ½ oz freeze-dried crab meat (rehydrated)
3. 1 cup mashed potatoes
4. 2 tbsp powdered whole milk
5. 1 tbsp breadcrumbs
6. 1 shallot
7. 2 tsp flour
8. 1 tsp fish seasoning
9. 2 tbsp grated freeze-dried parmesan cheese
10. 1 tbsp ghee
11. Salt & Pepper to taste

Method:

1. Add boiling water to the mashed potatoes and leave to one side.
2. In a pan melt the ghee.
3. Cook the onions in the ghee until see-through.
4. In a cup of water mix the milk and flour.
5. Add this to the pan, bring it to a boil, and stir.
6. Add salt and pepper according to taste.
7. Add the salmon & the crab meat and cook for a further minute or until the mixture thickens.
8. Transfer the mixture to 2 dishes and top with mashed potato.
9. Cover with the grated cheese and breadcrumbs. Enjoy!

Tuna, Rice & Veggie Pilaf

A tasty, healthy dish for the family to enjoy.

Prep Time: 10 mins Cook Time: 10-15 mins Serves: 1

Ingredients:

1. 4 oz. tuna
2. 1 tbsp freeze-dried beans(rehydrate)
3. 1 tbsp freeze-dried carrots(rehydrate)
4. 1 tbsp broth mix
5. 1 cup rice (white or brown)
6. 1 tbsp extra virgin olive oil
7. 1 tbsp freeze-dried parmesan cheese
8. Sea salt to taste

Method:

1. In a pot add 1 cup of water, tuna, vegetables, and oil, and bring to a boil.
2. Stir in the rice.
3. Remove from the heat and set to one side for 10 minutes.
4. Add the parmesan cheese.
5. Season to taste and enjoy!

Vegetarian Peppery Rice

A tasty filling nutritious meal.

Prep time: 30 mins Cook Time: 5 mins Serves: 1

Ingredients:

1. ½ cup freeze-dried rice
2. ¼ cup freeze-dried bell peppers
3. ¼ cup freeze-dried green-lentil chili
4. 1 tbsp freeze-dried zucchini
5. 1 tbsp freeze-dried carrots
6. 1 tbsp powdered tomato sauce
7. 2 cups water for rehydration

Method:

1. Add all the ingredients to a pot to soak.
2. Transfer to the stove and bring to a boil for 1 minute.
3. Add insulating cover to the pot and leave for 20 minutes.
4. Serve and enjoy!

Mushroom Penne

A tasty pasta packed full of flavor.

Prep time: 10 mins Cook Time:20 mins Serves:1 (Increase quantities to prepare a meal for 4)

Ingredients:

1. 1 cup penne pasta
2. 1/3 cup freeze-dried mushrooms
3. 2 tbsp freeze-dried carrots
4. 2 tbsp freeze-dried spinach
5. ½ cup freeze-dried onion
6. 2/3 cup powdered tomato
7. 1 tsp powdered garlic
8. 2 tsp dried cheese
9. 1 tsp sugar
10. 2 tbsp Italian seasoning
11. ¼ tsp marjoram
12. Pinch of thyme
13. ¼ tsp salt

Method:

1. Add all of the ingredients along with 4 ½- 5 cups of water to a deep pan and heat until simmering.
2. Simmer for around 15-20 minutes until the sauce thickens and the pasta is cooked. Stir frequently, adding extra water if required.
3. Serve in a bowl, super tasty!

Mango Salsa

A refreshing dish to have with tacos or as a side dish with your meal.

Prep time: 10 mins Serves: 1

Ingredients:

1. 2 cups of freeze-dried mangoes
2. ¼ cup diced tomato
3. ½ cup diced orange bell pepper
4. 1 tbsp diced jalapeno
5. 1/8 cup chopped red onion
6. 1/8 tsp Himalayan salt
7. ¼ cup cilantro
8. 1 tbsp lime juice
9. 2/3 cup water

Method:

1. Rehydrate the mangoes in a bowl of water.
2. In a separate bowl add together the peppers, tomatoes, onion, and jalapenos.
3. Drain the mangoes and add them to the vegetable mixture.
4. Add salt to taste, and chopped cilantro, and stir.
5. Mix in the lime juice and toss to cover the fruit and vegetables. Enjoy!

Muesli Bites

Bursting with fruits and nuts this tasty snack makes a great treat.

Prep time: 10 mins Cook Time: 15 mins Serves: 8

Ingredients:

1. 1 cup rolled oats
2. 1 cup unsweetened dried coconut
3. 1 cup unsweetened dried cranberries
4. ½ cup unsalted sunflower seeds
5. ½ cup unsalted raw pumpkin seeds
6. ¼ cup unsalted sesame seeds
7. ¼ cup flaxseeds
8. 1/3 cup wheat germ
9. ½ cup honey
10. 1/8 cup brown sugar
11. 7 tbsp butter, a few extra for cooking

Method:

1. Grease a 9-inch baking tray and line it with grease-proof paper.
2. In a large deep pan add the oats, coconut, wheat germ, sesame seeds, sunflower seeds and pumpkin seeds, and toast over medium heat until golden in color (around 8-10 mins).
3. Remove from the heat and move contents to a metal bowl to cool down.
4. Once cooled, add the cranberries and the flaxseeds.
5. Add the butter, sugar, and honey to a small pan and set to medium heat.
6. Stir until the sugar has dissolved (around 3-4 mins).
7. Boil and reduce to low heat to simmer for 5 mins. Do not stir.
8. Add this mixture to the bowl of dry ingredients and stir to mix.
9. Using a spoon add the mixture to the baking tray.
10. Ensure the mixture is pressed down evenly and firmly (this will ensure when it comes to cutting that perfect bars can be created, avoiding a crumbly mixture)
11. Leave to cool and cut into 8 tasty bars. Enjoy!

Raspberry Cheesecake Cookies

A tasty treat for the family

Prep time: 15 mins Cook time:12 mins Chill time: 2 hours Serves: 8

Ingredients:

1. 1 cup freeze-dried raspberries
2. 1 cup white chocolate chips
3. 2 ½ cups all-purpose flour
4. 1 cup unsalted butter
5. 6 oz cream cheese (room temperature)
6. 1 cup granulated sugar
7. 1 tsp vanilla
8. 1 egg yolk
9. ¼ tsp salt

Method:

1. In a large bowl add together the sugar, cream cheese, and butter. Mix with an electric mixer until light and fluffy.
2. Reducing to a low speed add the flour and fold in the raspberries and chocolate chips.
3. Cover and pop in the fridge for two hours.
4. Preheat oven to 375 degrees F/190 degrees C and line two baking trays with greaseproof paper.
5. Using 2 tbsp of dough, shape into balls and place them evenly apart on the trays, and flatten to form a circle.
6. Bake for 12-18 minutes until golden brown.
7. Transfer to wire racks to cool and enjoy!

Doughnuts with Raspberry Glaze

A tasty snack the family will enjoy.

Prep time: 5 mins Cook time: 12 mins Serves: 8

Ingredients:

Doughnuts:

1. 140 g plain flour
2. 1 tsp baking powder
3. 70 g caster sugar
4. 125 ml buttermilk
5. 1 egg
6. 3 tbsp raspberry juice
7. 1 tsp vanilla
8. 2 tbsp butter (melted and cooled)
9. 1 tbsp freeze-dried raspberries
10. ¼ tsp salt

Glaze:

1. 3 tbsp raspberry juice
2. 150 g powdered icing sugar

Topping:

1. 2 tbsp freeze-dried raspberries

Method:

1. Preheat the oven to 350 degrees F/160 degrees.C
2. Grease two 6-cup doughnut trays.
3. In a bowl mix together the vanilla, salt, baking powder, flour, and sugar.
4. In another bowl combine the raspberry juice, egg, and buttermilk.
5. Add the melted butter and the raspberries.
6. Mix the contents of the two bowls together.

7. Spoon this mixture into 8 doughnut cups in the doughnut trays to ¾ full.
8. Bake for 15 minutes, remove, cool and transfer to a wire rack to finish cooling.
9. For the glaze, combine the icing sugar and 1 tbsp of raspberry in a bowl.
10. Add a further tbsp of raspberries to thicken up the glace.
11. Dip the doughnuts into the glaze, add some freeze-dried raspberries and allow to set for 15 minutes before enjoying.

Apple Pie

Yummy apple pie, a favorite pie for the family.

Prep time: 20 mins Cook time: 1 hour Serves: 8

Ingredients:

Crust:

1. 1 tbsp butter
2. 2 ½ cups flour
3. 1 tbsp shortening
4. ½ cup shortening
5. 1 ½ sticks butter (sliced)
6. 1 tsp salt
7. Ice water

Filling:

1. 2 cups freeze-dried apples (sliced).
2. 2 tsp cinnamon
3. ¼ cup brown sugar
4. 1 tbsp vanilla
5. 1 tsp salt
6. 2 ½ cups water

Method:

1. In a large bowl add the flour, salt and shortening and mix until there are no lumps.
2. Blend in ½ stick of butter. Then add the rest of the butter, toss lightly, and squash the pieces flat.
3. Add around ½ cup of iced water until the mixture comes together.
4. Separate the mixture into 2 balls, flatten to a square shape, and chill for 60 mins.
5. Remove one from the fridge and roll out and place into a greased pie tin overlapping the edge by 2 inches and chill.

6. Add the apple, water, brown sugar, cinnamon, vanilla, and salt to a large bowl. Mix allowing the apple to rehydrate.
7. Add the filling to the pre-chilled base with 1 tbsp butter divided over the filling.
8. Roll out the second ball and lay over the filling, pinching the two crusts together. Make some holes in the top crust and chill for 30-60 mins.
9. Heat the oven to 425 degrees F and bake the pie for 15 mins. Lower the temperature to 350 degrees F and cook for a further 45 mins.
10. Leave to sit for an hour, slice, and enjoy!

Happy Freeze-Drying!

Although only a small selection of recipes (meals to make to freeze dry and those meals you can make with freeze-dried ingredients) have been chosen, I do hope this has inspired you to try some of these and armed with all the knowledge you have gained in the culinary art of freeze-drying that you will continue to experiment with your recipes and be prepared for the future.

Made in United States
Troutdale, OR
09/16/2024

22856314R10062